Is it Symmetrical?

Nancy Kelly Allen

ROURKE PUBLISHING
www.rourkepublishing.com

www.rourkepublishing.com

PHOTO CREDITS: Cover: Gennadiy Poznyakov, © Mike Bentley; Title Page: © Carmen Martínez Banús; Page 3: © Brent Hathaway, © Dominik Pabis, © Nina Shannon; Page 5: © Dominik Pabis; Page 7: © Ekaterina Monakhova, © Brent Hathaway; Page 8: © Scott Slattery; Page 9: © Pathathai Chungyam; Page 9, 10: © Maksim Inozemtsev; Page 11: © Tomasz Zachariasz, © Jesse Kunerth; Page 12: © Chepko Danil; Page 13, 14: © Sean Gladwel; Page 13: © Yuri Arcurs; Page 15: © Amanda Rohde, © Nina Shannon; Page 16: © Carrie Bottomley; Page 17: © Aaron Harewood, © Mariya Bibikova; Page 18: © Rainer von Brandis; Page 19, 21: © Liudmila Sundikova; Page 23: © Mariya Bibikova, © Maksim Inozemtsev, © Nina Shannon, © Tomasz Zachariasz

Edited by Kelli L. Hicks

Cover and Interior design by Tara Raymo

Library of Congress Cataloging-in-Publication Data

Allen, Nancy Kelly, 1949-
 Is it symmetrical? / Nancy Kelly Allen.
   p. cm. -- (Little world math concepts)
 Includes bibliographical references and index.
 ISBN 978-1-61590-297-2 (Hard Cover)(alk. paper)
 ISBN 978-1-61590-536-2 (Soft Cover)
 1. Symmetry (Mathematics)--Juvenile literature. I. Title.
 QA174.7.S96A55 2011
 516'.1--dc22
                                2010009639

Rourke Publishing
Printed in the United States of America, North Mankato, Minnesota
050511
050211LP-A

www.rourkepublishing.com - rourke@rourkepublishing.com
Post Office Box 643328 Vero Beach, Florida 32964

What in the world is symmetrical?

A leaf is symmetrical because the left half looks like the right half.

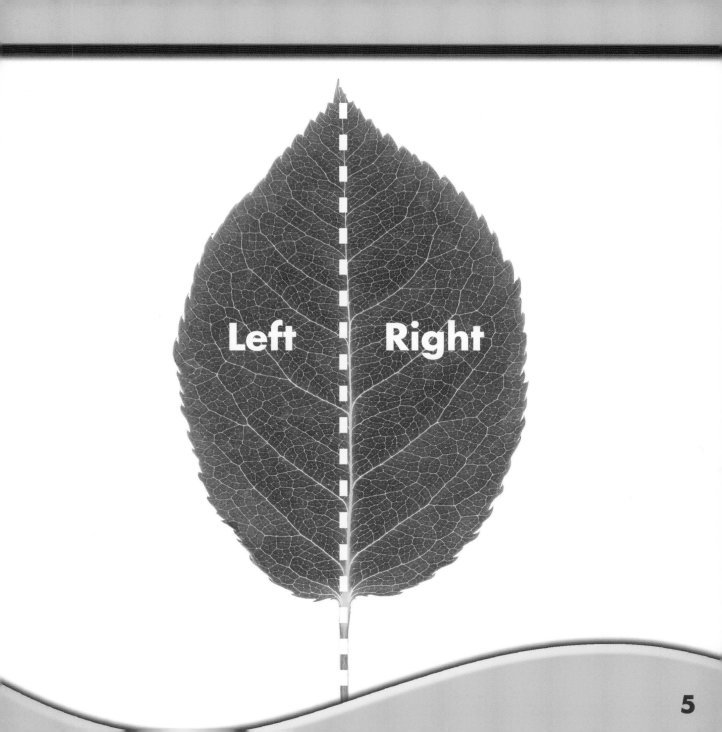

Left

Right

Is a butterfly symmetrical?

The left half looks like the right half.
A butterfly is symmetrical.

Is a pinecone symmetrical?

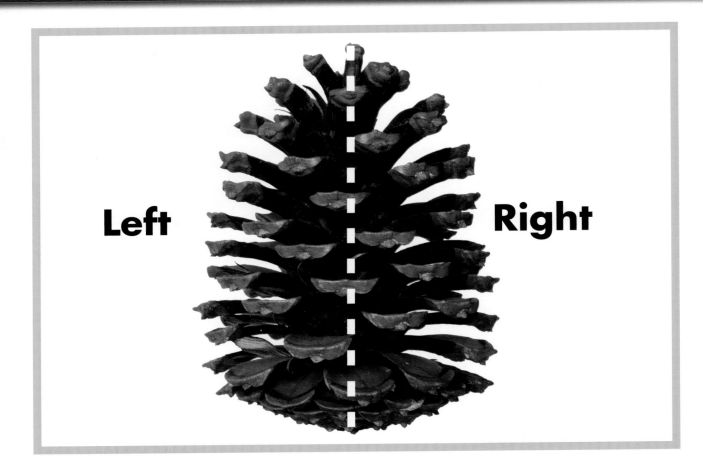

Left

Right

The left half looks like the right half.
A pinecone is symmetrical.

Is a ladybug symmetrical?

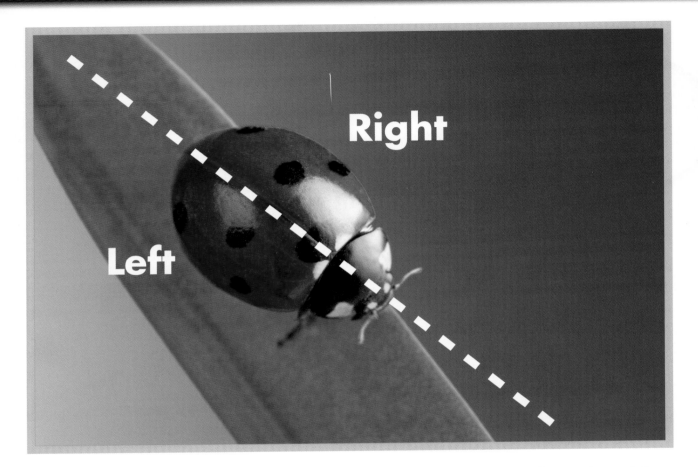

The left half looks like the right half.
A ladybug is symmetrical.

Is the cloud symmetrical?

The left half does not look like the right half. The cloud is not symmetrical!

Is the rock symmetrical?

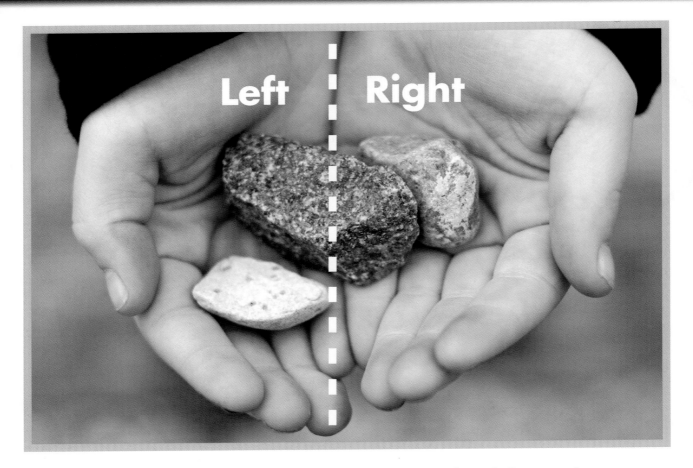

Left | Right

The left half does not look like the right half. The rock is not symmetrical!

Is the crab symmetrical?

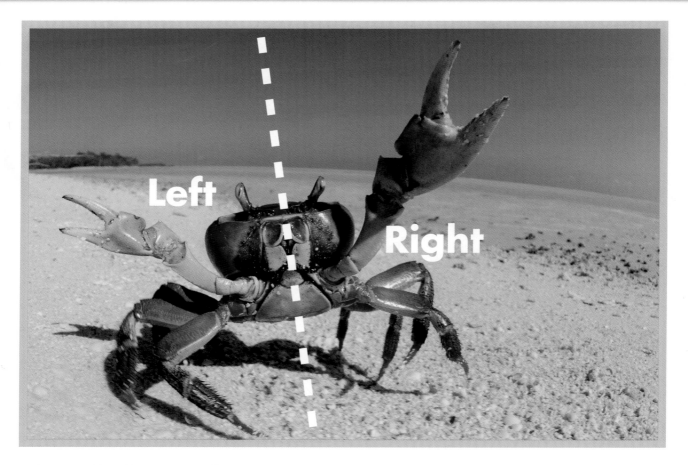

Left

Right

The left half does not look like the right half. The crab is not symmetrical!

Am I symmetrical?

The left half looks like the right half. Yes, I am symmetrical!

Can you find the things that
are symmetrical?

Index

Websites

www.boowakwala.com/kids/boowakwala-adventures-fingerpaint-symmetrypaint.html

www.haelmedia.com/OnlineActivities_txh/mc_txh4_001.html

www.adrianbruce.com/Symmetry/

About the Author

Nancy Kelly Allen lives in a log house in Kentucky. The logs are sawed, so the left half of each log looks like the right half. She lives with her husband, Larry, and two miniature schnauzers. Her schnauzers look like each other, but they don't look at all like Nancy.